The Write Habits – How To Write 2500 Words A Day

I0440437

Written by Zak Frazer

Copyright © Zak Frazer

For More Books,

Subscribe To My Mailing List – <u>*Click Here*</u>

Disclaimer:

This book has been produced for the Amazon Kindle and is distributed by Amazon Direct Publishing

Introduction

In 2014 I had the biggest wakeup call of my entire life – I had not accomplished even a fraction of the things I dreamt about.

Day in and day out I'd spend dreaming about being an accomplished writer, a vegetarian, travel to Greece and build a business online but none of those abovementioned dreams were actually coming true.

And it wasn't because of bad circumstances or whatever excuse I concocted over the years to make myself feel better – it was simply because I wasted a lot of time being someone who wants things easy rather than someone who is out there busting his ass to accomplish everything on his bucket list.

Wanting things and actually going out there, working hard and trying to get those things are two completely different things.

Having dreams are good but not doing anything about it is absolutely pointless.

And it was at that moment I realized the only person holding me back from accomplishing great things was me.

I got out of bed the next morning at 6am, grabbed my laptop and took a drive to the beach. I pulled up a blank page on Microsoft Word and wrote the following words – **I Am A Winner!**

It was at this point I completely discarded the way I lived life and got started on what I call – **The Ultimate Lifestyle.**

I wrote down exactly what I was going to do every single day, come hell or high water, and I would stick to this ultimate lifestyle until I struck off every last item on my bucket list.

It meant that I was literally going to start my business from scratch on that day – which I did! And every single day I would make an account of all the mini goals that were accomplished and make a new list before I started the next day.

On my list was writing 2500 words every single day for the rest of my life.

And you know what, since then I have published 7 books on Amazon and currently set a goal of writing and publishing 2 books a week for the entire year of 2015!

So before we get started on how you can write 2500 words daily, I want you to be prepared in every sense of the word for **work**! The idea that things can come easy in life is nothing more than a pipe dream.

And I can say that because I was that person who expected great results without putting in the hard work. If you live your life not willing to kick your own ass every single day in order to achieve your goals and dreams, I'm afraid you will find yourself living with regret when time has passed and you cannot get it back.

It's not too late though. If you commit yourself to making a positive change (buying this book is a testament to that commitment) and you give a 110% to everything that you do, I promise you that someday you will be extremely proud of all the things you've accomplished.

The very first lesson to this book is to be committed.

I want you to commit yourself to writing as much as you can no matter what happens. You find an hour every day and you write.

Even if it means sacrificing some leisure time or a bit of sleep, you write until you accomplish that daily goal. If you live with this hardworking mind-set, nothing will be able to hold you back from reaching and grabbing onto success.

Now, take a second to analyse how you spend your day. How much of it is actually spent being productive?

And I'm not talking about you loading yourself up with 100s of tasks but never actually finishing them.

I'm talking about the time you spend getting some proper work completed. Because at the end of the day, if something isn't completed, you never actually reach that level of success you desire.

A recipe that is missing the final ingredient will never be the dish you desired to make – neither will it taste as it's meant to.

So make a note of all the time you spend being productive and then on a separate page I want you to make a note of all the time you spend on mundane tasks.

Make a note of all the things that have no actual significance to your life.

Perhaps you watch days of our lives – *an hour a day spent watching a soapie that has zero impact on your life.* I mentioned this earlier, being productive is about completing tasks that have some sort of significance.

Even if it means breaking down a big task into smaller accomplishable goals – as long as it's going to be completed, it counts as being productive.

Afterwards, I want you to take a look at your mundane activity list and choose an item that you can remove and replace with your goal of writing. Life is all about prioritising and if we are unable to sacrifice our wants for our needs, we'd all end up bankrupt, unhealthy and on the verge of death.

It's not too much to ask of yourself to sacrifice just a single *want* that has no significance in your life and replace it with a craft that could possibly fulfil you in many different ways.

If you can successfully complete this one small task, I have no fear of you quitting this book because the first actions/the first step is often where most people fail and quit.

Take this one step and you will be on the train of success that only stops when it reaches its destination – right after it takes you on the best journey with the most spectacular views you've ever seen in your entire life!

Expelling A Lazy Mind-set

I can truly say, without a doubt in mind, that the single most difficult challenge for a writer to overcome is a lazy mind-set.

It is that kind of thinking that prohibits you from expanding your knowledge base and making an extra effort into finding your unique voice as a writer.

If you don't take that next simple step of opening an empty Microsoft Word document and writing the first word, you will never get to 2500 words a day.

As much as I hate sounding so pessimistic, it's just reality.

Unless you make a conscious effort of expelling all those negative and lazy thoughts from your mind, you will never accomplish a fraction of the dreams on your bucket list, period!

The only time for writing is ***right now***! Not later or any time after.

I set the goal of writing 2500 words daily and regardless of what happens I make sure to complete that goal. Forgot about everything else – focus on that one important mission – *writing 2500 words.*

I tend to implement *the punish or reward* system into my life.

If I don't complete my goal, I punish myself by switching all electronic devices off for an entire hour. It drives me crazy –

we all have become so dependent on technology that an hour away from the internet feels like a lifetime.

Not to mention I get bored as hell and by the end of that hour, I am literally dying to write!

So in a way, the idea of punishing myself has moulded me into someone who is a bit more disciplined.

And in cases where I complete my 2500 words a day goal and sometimes surpass that amount in one sit down, I reward myself with a single scoop of ice cream (I absolutely love vanilla flavoured ice cream).

The principle is just to discipline yourself and make yourself accountable for your actions.

As we get older we are afforded a new sense of freedom that keeps growing. Some of us are able to use that freedom to catapult our lives into great success and happiness whilst the majority of us tend to get laid back and lose interest in meeting deadlines and being responsible for our actions.

A writer's purpose is to write. You don't have to be published to call yourself a writer.

What makes you a writer, and a successful writer, is to set a goal to write for yourself and meet that goal every single day without fail.

That is what it means to be a writer (in my opinion).

I want you to realize that being lazy will get you absolutely zero results. It's not worth it.

All that effort you put into doing nothing would be better utilized for pursuing your dreams. The only thing that can truly hold you back from being a writer and a successful writer at that is laziness.

If you can dedicate yourself to completing a task, writing 2500 words daily, I guarantee you will be a whole lot happier when you look back at your accomplishments than had you remained a lazy slouch!

Developing A System

Through all my experience thus far as a writer, the biggest mistake I had made initially was not having a system in place.

A system involves taking a number of different steps towards ensuring that you can write as anticipated.

1. Choosing the perfect time to write
2. Finding the best location to write
3. Acquiring the essential information
4. Linking ideas and thoughts together
5. Having a rough sketch of the entire article/chapter
6. Writing

Establishing A Routine – Choosing The Perfect Time To Write

The art of building a habit entails practice. Are you a fan of the karate kid movies? Daniel san had to 'wax on and wax off' quite a bit before he could progress to the next level and so will you.

What many people fail to realize is that writing is more of a skill than an art. Through consistent practice, you too can become a qualitative and quantitative writer.

I would like for you to dedicate 25 minutes today, right now if possible, to simply write.

In that time I want you to write as much as you can about yourself as a person – your dreams, goals, failures, accomplishments, memories and feelings for the full 25 minutes.

Do your best to take absolutely no breaks and worry not about grammar or spelling. I recently learnt about the pomodoro (tomato) technique in which you set a timer for 25 minutes and you work as best as you can during those 25 minutes without a break.

At the end, you reward yourself with a 5 minutes break to grab a swing of water, eat something or simply get some fresh air before you reset the timer for another 25 minutes and proceed with your next short burst of work.

It works so well because generally the average person loses concentration, focus and momentum after a while of working and ends up in a burnt out zone unable to continue.

The pomodoro technique remedies this problem and instead of you entering a burnt out zone after 60 minutes of working continuously without a break, you enter a 'burn out' zone in which you can push to the max for a sessions of 25 minutes of work at a time and then follow it up with 5 minutes of rest to recover, relax and reset your focus for another round.

But that's not all;

I want you to choose a time in your day when you feel your absolute best. It could be very early in the morning before the sun even rises or it could be late at night when all that surrounds you is silence and an eerie feeling of darkness.

The reason for this is actually to do with our psychological makeup – when you have to get up early in the morning, a time which you hate to spend anywhere but in your bed, and forced to go outside, sooner or later you're going to dislike being outside.

But in contrast, if you were to write during a time when you feel exceptionally awesome, your subconscious will eventually associate that awesome feeling with the task of writing!

So every time you write, you are going to be reminded of that positive emotions and it's going to help you push forward and write as best as you can!

Needless to say, a once off attempt at writing when you feel good isn't actually going to cut it, what becomes important at this point is following up on this little technique every single day.

However, the biggest problem many of us writers face is actually being able to convert our thoughts into words.

I want you to think about this for a second – *writing does not occur the second your fingers hit the keyboard*. The actual moment of writing is when you form a thought, ponder about it and draw other associated thoughts to it creating a mental spider diagram and actually knowing what you want to write about before you physically start writing. So in reality, writing takes place long before you have anything on paper. We'll get into the research part of this book soon, but first…

Choosing The Best Location For Writing:

I love being out in nature.

There's something relaxing and rejuvenating about being outside in the early morning of summer. Without a doubt, it's the one place that allows me to think of everything that matters to me and it just so happens that writing in this setting allows me to kind of meditate and relax.

In a way, writing is therapeutic to me. It contributes to my wellbeing and in turn that positive feeling allows me to write at my best.

I want for you to take some time and get a feel for writing in different spots. Perhaps you like writing in your bed at night or at a work desk as it enhances the principle of '*Get Shit Done*'!

The purpose of finding an ideal location is to ensure that you don't look for any external element to distract or disturb you from focussing on what needs to be done – **writing**?

Another reason is that the environment in which we find ourselves in tends to impact on the way we think and feel, thus it has a direct influence on what we end up writing.

In saying that, an ideal location is a place that enhances your positive emotions, helps you concentrate, eliminates any modern external factors that may distract you and it has many qualities that evoke motivation and potential ideas.

This brings me to an exceptionally important section of this book:

Acquiring Essential Information - Research

I asked you to write as much as you can about yourself for a period of 25 minutes for a reason – I know for a fact that you won't be able to write everything that enters your mind during that short session because you know yourself **completely**.

If anything I bet you could spend days writing about yourself and your life.

So have you considered the simple fact that you're unable to write about a specific topic, not because you're suffering from writers block or you're stuck in a rut, but because you have insufficient information to work with.

So the very first step to writing 2500 words a day is implementing a laser focussed method of researching information on what you want to write about.

You can do this by drawing as much information from your mind as possible and writing them down in a linear format on a page (in other words, make a list). Afterwards I want you to focus on the very first point on your list and ask yourself 4 questions:

- What does it mean?
- Where did it originate?
- How can it be used?
- Why is it important?

If you are unable to answer any of those questions, fire up Google and do a quick search or pull out a book that can help guide you. Read up on it until you feel familiar with the importance, usefulness and significance behind the first point we focussed on and try linking it to the second point.

Do this by asking the same 4 questions to your next point and continue until you find yourself with over a butt load of information that can be used by you to write a splendid article or chapter.

The very same principle can be applied for works of fiction.

For someone writing a book, write down the essence of the chapter in one paragraph and start making a list of all the events you want to unfold during the next set of pages. Ask yourself the 4 questions I mentioned above, build on your own thoughts and create a source of information within your mind that can be used to pen the chapter.

It will always boil down to how knowledgeable and familiar you are with the information needing to be written.

For someone writing fiction, if you spend a large amount of time simply thinking and understanding the reasons for why your characters act in a certain way and why certain events must take place, it would become insanely easy for you to write without getting stuck every few minutes.

But we know that writing isn't just about putting words onto a page, it entails magnificent amount of thought and logic before any of it can make sense.

No matter what a person may argue, it always comes back to research.

If you as a writer have a passionate interest about running and you've spent countless hours and days reading up different studies on the effects running has on the human physique and you actually physically keep in shape by running as often as you can –

- Wouldn't you be able to make sense of running on a much deeper level than someone who has zero interest in it?
- Wouldn't you be able to draw a connection between running and hormones that evoke positive feelings?
- Wouldn't you be able to identify common and uncommon issues that someone may face by or whilst running?
- Wouldn't you be able to give a long list of reasons as to the benefits running has on a person's overall health?

Yes you would!

But someone who has zero running and avoids it like the plague isn't going to even scratch the surface of running if he/she has hardly any theoretical, let alone physical experience of the topic.

Thus, if I were to place my money on who would write a spectacular book in the fastest amount of time, my money is going to be on the person who loves running!

This brings me to a very important point – research entails active participation.

If you want to write about something for hours on end and be able to churn out something of a high calibre, the most important decision you can make is finding a reason for you to either love it or hate it.

Activate Different Senses

After the last section, we can safely say that it is an established fact that the reason why many of us struggle to meet our writing quota for a day or week is because we lack the necessary information and understanding about a particular topic.

I mentioned earlier that a writer needs to immerse himself into the subject matter and become familiar with all the characteristics that make up the central theme of a story or situation.

An amazing way of improving your skills as a descriptive writer and one that is able to recreate an image through words is by activating your own senses before and whilst writing.

Let's say I wanted to paint a picture for you of the beach. I could easily sit at my desk and try to draw as many characteristics synonymous with the beach and try to word a descriptive paragraph. I'm not saying it won't be good but it could turn into a difficult feat if you haven't been to the beach in years and don't have a particular liking to it.

But if I were to actually visit the beach, walk amongst the cheerful sun kissed faces at the beach, grab grains of warm sand with the grooves of my toes and smell the salty cold breeze that bites at my skin – wouldn't I be able to compose an exceptionally fantastic piece about the beach? I sure would!

Sometimes the best form of writing is one from experience.

I've seen many writers pen an entire fictional environment setting that was inspired from a trip to Netherlands or The North Pole.

Your greatest asset is your ears, eyes, mouth and limbs.

With them you can experience the true nature of an object and environment to the extent of being able to describe elements that a common writer may miss.

If anything, activating your different senses and experiencing a particular thing live is one of the best ways to acquire information. That is why I still prefer to visit the library and pick out a few books on cooking or business.

Being able to feel the pages, smell the scent of a new/old book and read out loud whilst having those other senses active promotes my understanding and liking of a topic – regardless of how boring I may have once found it to be!

The next time you find yourself battling to get started on a specific topic, search for different way to activate your senses and learn more about it. You could fire up YouTube and search for a few videos on the topic – that will activate both your senses of sight and hearing. You could ask someone in person and have them share some of their knowledge on the matter to you.

Knowledge is the most powerful tool a writer can have. If you spend just as much time learning as you do writing, you'll find that you have successfully built two habits that are dependent on each other and promote the level of efficiency at which you work.

Make it a side by side goal to read 2 pages of a book every single day!

At the end of a week, pull up a blank document and write a 2500 words essay of the 14 pages you read over the last 7 days. Guaranteed you will have no problem doing so and may even enjoy the process.

Identity Transformation

Essentially, this book is a guide centred on helping you build a new habit. What I have encountered over the years personally is that most habits don't stick.

Some may say it has a lot to do with motivation whereas others claim it relates to a lazy mind-set but there's another factor that is often overlooked – **focussing on results.**

We take on a new habit because it presents us with the prospect of gain. Lifting weights results in muscle gain, running daily results in greater fat loss and writing daily gains us experience, speed and efficiency (and not forgetting a completed project that could gain us money, fame and recognition).

Habits don't stick if the only reason for it is gaining a result – the correct approach is an identity transformation. Being the version of yourself who makes you happy and positive is what makes a habit stick.

If you view yourself as a lazy slouch, it's likely that you'd build habits that promote such an identity.

You would spend most of your free time on the couch catching up on soapies whilst snacking on a huge bar of chocolate and sipping on a full cream latte.

However, if you view yourself as an efficient writer, you would act accordingly and build a long term habit of writing a certain amount of words every day and presenting a quality of work that you view as praiseworthy.

So simply writing 2500 words a day for the sake of completing a book or making money won't last long term.

The only way to actually create a solid habit built on a foundation that can withstand other contrasting negative habits is to change your identity. Instead of setting a goal of writing to finish a book, set a goal of writing 2500 words a day to become **an efficient writer** *(this is just one type of identity a writer can have, you can do it for many other identity types).*

Let your goals help craft you into the best version of yourself.

Cutting Back On External Factors

From this point onwards, I want you to focus on the stuff that is a priority to your existence. You wouldn't go a day without eating food and you'd find the time to make or purchase the meal you crave.

Similarly, you wouldn't hold your breath every second minute because breathing itself is essential to your existence.

So if you can make writing a survival priority – something which you simply cannot live without, can you imagine the amount of books and amazing articles you will be able to write in one lifetime?

I can't imagine because it would be humungous.

And I believe that-that is the difference between modern day authors and those legendary authors from the past – we view writing as a means to an end whereas they viewed writing as a means to survival.

We look at the possibility of getting published so that we can earn lots of money, acquire fame and be glorified by people around the world but many of the authors that have penned content that has outlived them wrote for the sole purpose of just writing out of pure passion and love for what they wrote about.

If you truly want to write the best 2500 words of your life every single day, then I suggest you write because you either love the process of writing or the topic you wish to write about.

Nevertheless, the best way to avoid losing out on precious time and words is to eliminate any external element that can draw your attention away from the task at hand.

1. Log Off All Social Networking Accounts

Unless what you are writing about deals directly with social networking, it is a must that you shut down all social networking accounts for each session of writing.

You see, when we end up riding a train of a particular thought, if you get distracted and knocked off that train, it's extremely difficult to get back on it. That's when you find yourself staring at a paragraph unable to link ideas together.

From here on out, whenever you plan on dedicating a full 25 minutes to writing, log off and let your brain focus on what's important.

I remember watching Sherlock Holmes and he mentioned choosing the kind of information he wanted his brain to absorb – anything that wasn't relevant to the topic at hand was useless to him in that moment and he had no intention of consuming any piece of information that didn't piece together the puzzle in his mind.

To be brutally honest, Facebook is completely saturated with the most random information you can find in the whole internet!

Three quarter of what you read on Facebook will provide absolutely no benefit to your life and yet we allow our brain to use up space and consume irrelevant information.

For what reason?

Will it make us better writers? Will it provide us with a treasure chest of relevant information? Will it make us better human beings who are superbly productive? No!

It's pointless – at least for someone trying to meet a goal of writing thousands of words a day!

2. Avoid Multitasking

It was only recently that I discovered how multi-tasking is nothing more than a fancy word for being a jack of all trades and a master at none!

Why is it that we focus on doing multiple things at once and not completing anything?

Let's say you multitask by writing 5 stories at the same time. That means you are putting in 20% of effort per story and it takes you 5 days to complete all 5 stories. However, if you were to give 100% to a single story, you would write that story 5 times faster and finish it in a single day.

In 5 days you would still have 5 stories completed! So this whole concept of multitasking is just a term used by people who are unorganized and unwilling to give a 100% effort to a single task to trick themselves into thinking that they are being productive.

In hindsight it looks as though you're working faster and getting more done but it's nothing more than an illusion which has a greater risk rather than return!

Let's say you quit writing at the end of day 3 after trying the whole concept of multitasking. That would mean you have 5 stories that are 40% short of being complete whereas if you followed the system of applying a 100% focus to a single story, you'd have 3 books already completed and in the bag!

I strongly recommend focusing all your attention to one topic or article at a time. If you set out to write 7 articles or chapters that are 2500 words, don't write tid-bits of each chapter. It's okay if you want to jump between article/chapter 2 to 5 and then back to 1 provided you actually complete a chapter from start to finish.

It will take a bit more dedication and commitment but in the end you are actually getting things done and are actually completing stuff which to me is an accomplishment on its own. That gives you a right to actually feel proud of yourself!

3. Criticism From Others

We writers generally look for an outside analysis to get an idea of what message is being related to the reader – however the reaction we get isn't always a positive one and neither is it something we anticipate.

No writer submits a piece of work expecting it to be panned by readers.

We generally prefer releasing stuff that is either close to perfect in our own eyes or at the very least adequate.

However, I find myself getting extremely worked up over an idea and I get ahead of myself. The excitement overwhelms me and I tend to reveal my incomplete story or article to someone for an opinion because in my head I know how amazing the finish product is going to be.

What I find is that sometimes I don't get the outstanding reaction I expect.

That brings me to another point – ***don't have unrealistic expectations from others***. Art is completely subjective. What I may find to be spectacularly beautiful, you may find it to be boring and dull.

And writing is a **form of Art**. The quote '*one man's meat is another man's poison*' comes to mind.

The only person's approval you should be focussed on when trying to build a habit such as this is your own.

I touched on developing your identity as a writer.

If you don't see yourself as an efficient and amazing writer, it won't matter what others say, your inner belief will be lacking and you'd never be able to break free and write as much as you want.

In my humblest of opinions, I suggest you avoid revealing work that isn't complete until you are comfortable with your identity as a writer. Build some momentum and let the words that appear on your page inspire you before you look for an outside stimulus to provide that extra assurance.

Disappointing Comparisons

We live in a time where people are compared against each other to determine who is better than the other.

It's unfortunate that this reality we have created is willing to base our efforts on the opinions of others or biased statistics.

You are a writer.

The second you convert a thought into a sentence, you have become a writer. How good or bad of a writer you are should be decided by comparing yourself to a version of you from yesterday.

Essentially, your only competitor to beat is yourself and the comparisons you draw between the version of you from yesterday and the version of you from today are much more valuable than the standard comparisons people choose to draw between different writers.

Who do you write for?

Your first answer should be yourself. The second should be for readers. With that in mind, who do you think is the best person to judge your improvement against? The answer is **You!**

Unless you can find a writer who is a clone of yourself and has the same thoughts, troubles and obstacles that you have, no one else can provide you with a fair comparison. I don't ever compare myself to other writers.

If I do, it would strip me of my freedom to grow.

By aiming to meet the standard of another writer, you are inherently accepting that he or she is superior than you and at a level of perfection that you would like to reach.

Some may argue that it's a good thing and don't get me wrong, having an idol who you look up to and want to write like is definitely something I support. But if you are starting out and you are comparing yourself to such a person and basing the future of your venture as a writer on such comparison, you are treading on dangerous grounds!

More importantly, you are jeopardizing your own writer's persona.

We all are unique, right? It's why one can decipher between a man written article and a robotic computerised article? Unlike a computer, we don't work with algorithms and formula's per say. Our personality is bound to influence the way in which we write. It's why I strongly believe that every writer has uniqueness to their writing that makes them special.

But when you start comparing your work to someone else, it's possible that you might want to emulate that person's way of writing.

Eventually you may successfully write like such person but that would simply make you a copycat – regardless of how splendid your work is.

Write for yourself. Let your personality contribute to the tone, flow and construction of your writing. This way of thinking will help you tremendously because then writing will merely become an extension of your personality, making it much easier for you to express yourself through the medium of written words.

Someday when you are dead and gone, your unique work will live for years to come.

It will be the legacy that reminds the world of your existence. Who knows, you could someday become the Shakespeare of the next century!

For the time being, avoiding comparisons will save you any disappointment and you will always be trying to simply beat yourself. To me, that's a fantastic way for a writer to grow and prosper. You can absolutely have goals to succeed like other writers and to be inspired by them, to use their achievements as motivation to say –'*that if they can do it, so can I*'. In that respect, looking up to other writers is a marvellous thing to do!

Always think that you are one step behind your best self. In that way, you will always want to chase after the best version of yourself and though you may always be one step behind, you will reach heights not even your idol can – let that sink in!

Reverse Quantity Writing Method

The standard technique of writing 2500 words entails breaking up your quota in to small chunks throughout the day.

A typical division would be 500 words spread out over 5 hours!

However, my mood impacts the way I write. Sometimes I start the day feeling insanely inspired and could easily push out 1500 words within an hour or 2. I tried the 500 word breakdown and it does work but on some days I get completely burnt out and then I find myself staring at the screen struggling to push out that remaining small quota.

In saying that, you could easily try the Reverse Quantity Writing Method.

That means writing 1250 words during your first sit down. Follow that up later on in the day with 750 words and towards the night you can write the last 500 words.

My energy levels helped me realize how this way of writing made more sense.

We start our days fuelled with loads of energy but as the night creeps in, we're left with just measly 10 – 20% energy until our body needs to shut down and sleep in order to recover.

So try writing the most you can during your most energetic time of the day and then lower amount of words you need to write at the next session.

And on some days, write whenever the hell you feel like it provided you meet that goal. It is currently 10:26 pm at night and I'm busy at my desk writing this section of the book whereas the day before I completed my 2500 words at 5pm!

It all depends on how you feel provided you meet that amount every single day without fail.

Needless to say, if you are someone who works better with a strict system in place and prefer to follow the standard 500 words an hour system until you meet your quota, go for it!

Over time your body and mind will become accustomed to this routine and if you try skipping a session, you'd end up feeling like something is wrong and your day is incomplete!

That is when you know that writing has become more than a habit – it has become a part of your lifestyle!

The Hateful Timer

At soccer camp, our coach used to follow a particular regiment called the hateful timer. He was well aware of how much we hated to do push ups so to 'motivate' us he would set a timer and ask us to complete 5 laps around the school grounds.

If we were unsuccessful at finishing all 5 laps before the timer hit zero, we would all have to spend the rest of practice doing push ups to failure!

And I tell you what, we all run as though our lives depended on it. It's like adrenalin kicked in and all we could think about was that finish line and not doing those dreaded push ups no matter what!

After a few weeks, not only did we always finish those 5 laps but our time of completion actually improved!

I experimented with this technique and found that my time for completing my quota of words improved.

Currently, I hate having to listen to heavy metal music. It makes me grind my teeth. So I set a time for myself and an amount of words to complete before my time runs out and I get cracking.

Just like my days at soccer training, I generally finish with time to spare and have actually witnessed an improvement in the amount of words I can write in 25 minutes.

On a side not, the amount of words I can type per minute also shot up. Not only am I capable of typing very efficiently but I can do so without looking at the keyboard at all!

This little technique is somewhat a spin off from **the punish and reward system** except this is focussed on improving the speed in which you write! What you can do is think about all the things you absolutely hate with all your being and make a list of them.

Set your timer and simply start writing.

If you are unable to meet the required amount of words, partake in any of the things you hate doing! This will discipline you and motivate you to work harder the next time round.

I understand that it can be a rather strict and annoying approach to writing faster but it does work and you are only improving your ability to work under different conditions and moods.

So even if you feel burnt out or demotivated, you will still end up writing that required amount of words every day to avoid doing any of the things you hate at all costs.

Write To Be Free

As a teen I always searched for something that could make me feel free. Everything and everyone around me were somehow subjected to different forms of control and not many people were actually truly free to discover themselves and what makes them happy!

I tried many different things like playing soccer again, pursuing drama class, listening to different genres of music but nothing made me feel unconditionally free.

It was only until we were tested in English to write a 350 word descriptive essay that included the sentence – *and the thumbtacks pressed against the paper*. Before I knew it, I was completely consumed in writing a story of a schizophrenic murderer!

Never in my teen life did I feel so free. Whenever I wrote, it felt like no one in the world could control my thoughts. I was free to write whatever the hell I wanted and it made me feel like a king!

If you need just one reason to write, let it be for freedom. You have the power to turn any thought in your mind into a piece of art and literature. No one in the world can control what you write on that page because it belongs to you and you alone.

Writing can offer you the feeling of control that has been stripped away from us as we got older and life started demanding more of our attention, energy and feelings!

The next time you think about writing, I want you to remember that writing gifts you freedom.

Changing Your Perspective

I'm going on a limb here and generalising that everyone likes to watch movies – including you.

Have you ever felt like spending an hour plus on a movie as a chore? Do you sit there impatiently waiting for the movie to end? Do you hit fast forward through the entire movie so that you can save time? No!

If anything, you sometimes wish a particular movie was longer, I know I do. So why is it that we struggle to look at writing in the same light that we do movies?

Perhaps the problem is our perspective on things. At times I can say that I'm guilty of approaching writing as a work – it happens to the best of us.

I get so fixated on the end result that the longer it takes me to write a particular book or chapter, the more frustrated and uninspired I become.

It feels like we start convincing our subconscious to view writing as work rather than a passion. And we've heard many people say that it's not work when you love what you're doing. So if we truly fall in love with writing at the dawn of every new day, perhaps writing large quantities would be a pleasure and completely easy to accomplish.

Heck you could end up sitting in front of your TV screen hoping for the movie to end so that you can get back to writing!

Ask yourself this – *why do I want to write*?

I said it before and I'm going to say it again – write because it helps you create your best identity. Look at yourself through the eyes of someone you view as important and ask yourself how you would want to be seen?

As a person who has become productive, happy, motivated and successful all because he loves to spend his days and nights writing or as a person who is forcing himself to write to gain something in return?

Look at writing as an extension of your personality.

Let it become the part of you that make you feel complete as a person. Allow it to completely transform your life into one that is full of accomplishments and happiness.

All that can be possible if you start to look at writing as something that promotes you as an individual!

Going Back In Time

Technology has come a far way over the last decade. It plays an exceptionally important part of our lives and has made it possible for every one of us to have our work published online and read by people all around the world.

It was a magnificent development and writers are now capable of accessing a butt load of tools and resources to enhance our abilities and promote our work.

But even technology has its flipside.

Being exposed to such an abundance of resources is beginning to overwhelm many of us. As an internet marketer, I had to spend a lot of my time understanding how people react online and my job was to establish different ways to make people click on different call to actions.

In other words, conversion rate optimization was to become my forte. What I learnt is that if you give people too many choices, they will often become completely overwhelmed and indecisive. In the end, they leave your page and take none of the many choices you offered.

So instead, it was advised that you make the choice for your potential buyers or subscribers. Limit the amount of action they can take on your page and monitor the results.

And guess what, results improved almost immediately. Sometimes, less is more!

Which brings me to my point – if you find that whenever you power up your laptop or PC, open up Google to search for different references and information only to end up overwhelmed and completely distracted on sites like 9Gag and Facebook, it may be a good idea for you to shift your writing to an environment with less choices.

What I mean by this is choosing to write offline. I sometimes take an old fashion approach to writing with a notepad and pen! I throw myself onto the couch, put on my thinking cap and start writing down all the important points that pop into my head.

It's proven to be quite an effective technique for me.

Watching a real blank page begin to fill up with ideas and thoughts that interconnect with each other and create a personal resource for me to reference when actually writing the first draft of my book inspires me and forces me to focus at the task at hand – writing!

But like I said, technology does offer many valuable resources so I decided to include 3 of them that I use regularly below:

1. Hemingway App – This nifty app flags overly long to difficult sentences as well as grammatical mistakes.

2. 750 Words – Helps you turn your writing into a game. As you write, you earn points and complete tasks. It's quite a fun way to write if you're struggling with it at first.

3. Written Kitten – I love using this website because after ever 100 words an entertaining – usually funny – picture of a cat pops up. I personally love cats so this website is just a creative way to work towards funnier and cuter cat pictures!

Stop Being A Perfectionist

Though editing forms part of the process of writing, it can easily be separated and that's what I've done with my own work. I'm not claiming that every piece of content that I've written over the last year has been a masterpiece built on perfection but the fact that I have published my work, learnt from my mistakes and improved myself as a writer in such a short space of time is a clear indication that what counts more than a godlike edited article is progress.

Some authors never ever publish their work because they can't seem to reach that level of perfection they so desperately desire.

If you are amongst that group, I suggest you think long and hard about where perfection has gotten you as a writer because time waits for no man and if you continuously hold yourself back, you will never grow as a writer.

I believe that no writer should or will ever reach a status of perfection.

Because if we did, then how does one ever grow past that point? How will you and I ever reach a higher status if we reach the top?

I don't want to stop trying to find perfection.

I know that I may live my entire life chasing after it but I can honestly say that I won't have any regret because I will reach a huge amount of accomplishments during my race to win perfection.

And that will only be possible if I were to actually write, complete and publish all the little pieces of art through the years.

Waiting until you can write that one poem, novel or story that is utterly perfect may never come – so do you want to spend the rest of your life as someone who chased perfection without having the courage of releasing the work you've already done or do you want to be someone who chased perfection and was courageous enough to publish his/her work and allowed it to be viewed as perfect by others around the world?

My point is that regardless of whether or not you view something as perfect, there may always be a reader out somewhere in the middle of nowhere who may stumble across what you wrote and think of it as the most perfect piece of literature on the planet!

I don't know about you but that makes me feel extremely warm and fuzzy on the inside. That alone is reason enough for me to work day in and day out in order to provide someone else with a small piece of perfection.

From here on out, **eliminate this stop and edit way of writing**. Write until you meet your daily quota and only afterwards should you attempt to edit. I notice people get caught up in the web of perfect edit and spend precious time trying to perfect a single small paragraph rather than writing all that they can and then proceeding to edit.

The entire point of editing is to enhance the original draft to a state of betterment and 'perfection'. How can you actually do that if you don't actually complete the draft?

How Long Will It Take You?

Obviously it would take a lot of work before you meet that actual goal of 2500 words a day but you have to start somewhere. Realistically speaking, you may not always meet that quota but the entire point of this habit is the process of it, not the result.

2500 words is just a result, the process is building the habit by writing.

Enjoy that process more than what you have to gain from it – even if the result will be that book you have spent your entire life dreaming about writing!

It's an awesome feeling knowing that by dedicating yourself to such a number of words every day in a row can bring you some of the most fantastic results in your entire life. And I truly do encourage you to focus on that but to a limited extent.

The majority of your attention should be spent on enjoying the process of writing. A habit is something that you can do regularly without much pain and suffering – right?

Or at the very least, that pain and suffering becomes the most enjoyable feeling you experience and you welcome the hard work!

But habits take time to develop and stick. It takes consistent effort and a conscious effort towards doing it. A person ought not to read for the sake of saying that he or she reads.

One should read for the purpose and process of acquiring knowledge and understanding key ideas in the text.

Similarly, this habit of writing should be all about enjoying the art of writing. The process of thinking of ideas that complement and contrast with each other and converting such thoughts into words and then a sentence and then a chapter and finally a book that is built on passion and critical thinking.

Dedicate at least a full month to building the habit of writing and have mini goals. I planned this book around the thought that you want to write 2500 words today and that's how I went about advising you but if you want to take a more realistic or slower route, it's completely okay.

I told you, it's not just about the destination, it's about the journey!

An alternate approach would be this: **Set out 28 days of your life towards making writing a habit that sticks!**

Start your first week with a small and achievable goal – 500 words. Stick to everything I mentioned previously about finding the perfect time to write, a suitable environment, your best mood and a topic that you're passionate about or very knowledgeable about – like yourself and your own life.

Spend the first week breaking out of a routine-less lifestyle and create a space in your day for writing and completely give yourself to the craft for that period of time.

If you manage to write 500 words for more than 5 days and it begins to feel easy and you time of completion improves, bump it up by another 500.

Keep this steady increase after every 5 days. You'll find that by day 25, you are pushing out a total of 2500 words a day. It is at this point that you continue aiming higher!

Now go to 3000 words and then to 3500!

The reason for this is simple. If you reach the point of being able to write way over 2500 words daily, even if you don't meet a particular high number, you will always meet that 2500 words a day goal.

That's the beauty of aiming higher than normal. Even if you don't meet that high standard, you will always reach that beginner goal you set for yourself and this habit will be one that sticks for life!

In Conclusion

It's usually the things that don't come easy in life that bring about the most happiness.

Perhaps it will take a lot of effort and hard work, gruelling hours in front of your computer screen and many hours spent researching and reading but that's just the beautiful madness of writing.

What many never get to experience is that **special feeling** when you accomplish that goal and write something you feel extremely proud off.

All that hard work and effort fades away in a second and you end up feeling like a king or queen!

Writing can truly be the most freeing craft in the entire world and it will always be in your control. Every word and every sentence will always belong to you and no one in the world can take away that piece of art that has your name written all over it.

Set achievable goals for yourself but always aim high. Building a habit simply entails consistency and persistence.

Keep on writing even with the results are nowhere in sight. Often it's those invisible benefits that accumulate over time and smack you in the face after weeks of hard work. And somehow it always turns out being better than anything you could have possibly imagined.

Let me tell you something, the fact that you put in the time and effort to read this compact guide from start to finish is a testament to your resolve and it's an accomplishment in its own right.

We covered how research and knowledge empowers a writer to be efficient and thought provoking, right?

Now that you have accomplished reading this guide and acquiring information as to how you can write more efficiently, are you ready to put your new found knowledge to use? Hell Yes!

To conclude, I would like to congratulate you and wish you luck on your future as a 2500 words a day writer! Be the person who chases after their dreams with everything in your being.

Don't let insecurities hold you back from being the best version of yourself. Channel that inner resolve within you and free your true identity – a person who always gets up no matter how many punches are thrown at you!

Stick to your guns and write for as long and as much as you can. Write until it consumes you and write for the beauty of writing.

In the end, 2500 words won't even be a challenge for you – that's my personal guarantee to you!